EXILE & the PROPHETIC

IMAGES FROM THE NEW DIASPORA

Marc H. Ellis

WIPF & STOCK · Eugene, Oregon

Wipf and Stock Publishers
199 W 8th Ave, Suite 3
Eugene, OR 97401

Exile & the Prophetic
Images from the New Diaspora
By Ellis, Marc H.
Copyright©2015 by Ellis, Marc H.
ISBN 13: 978-1-4982-4511-1
Publication date 3/20/2017
Previously published by New Dispora Books, 2015

For my father

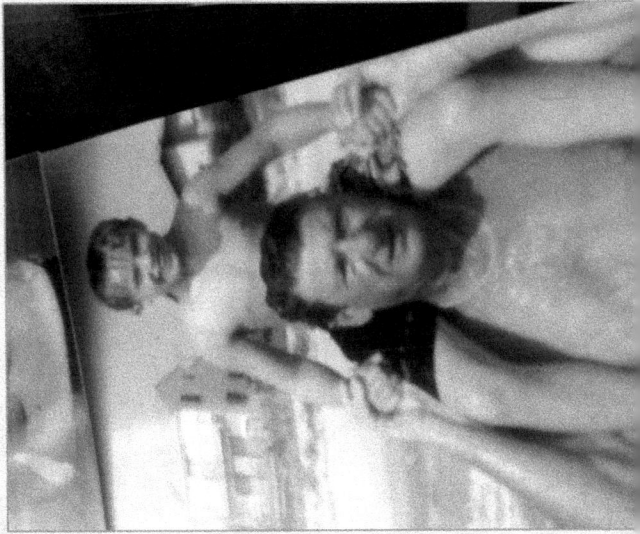

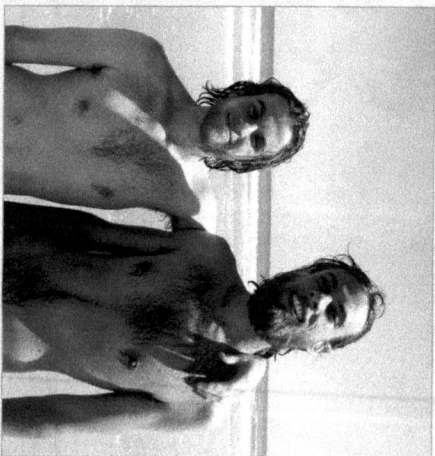

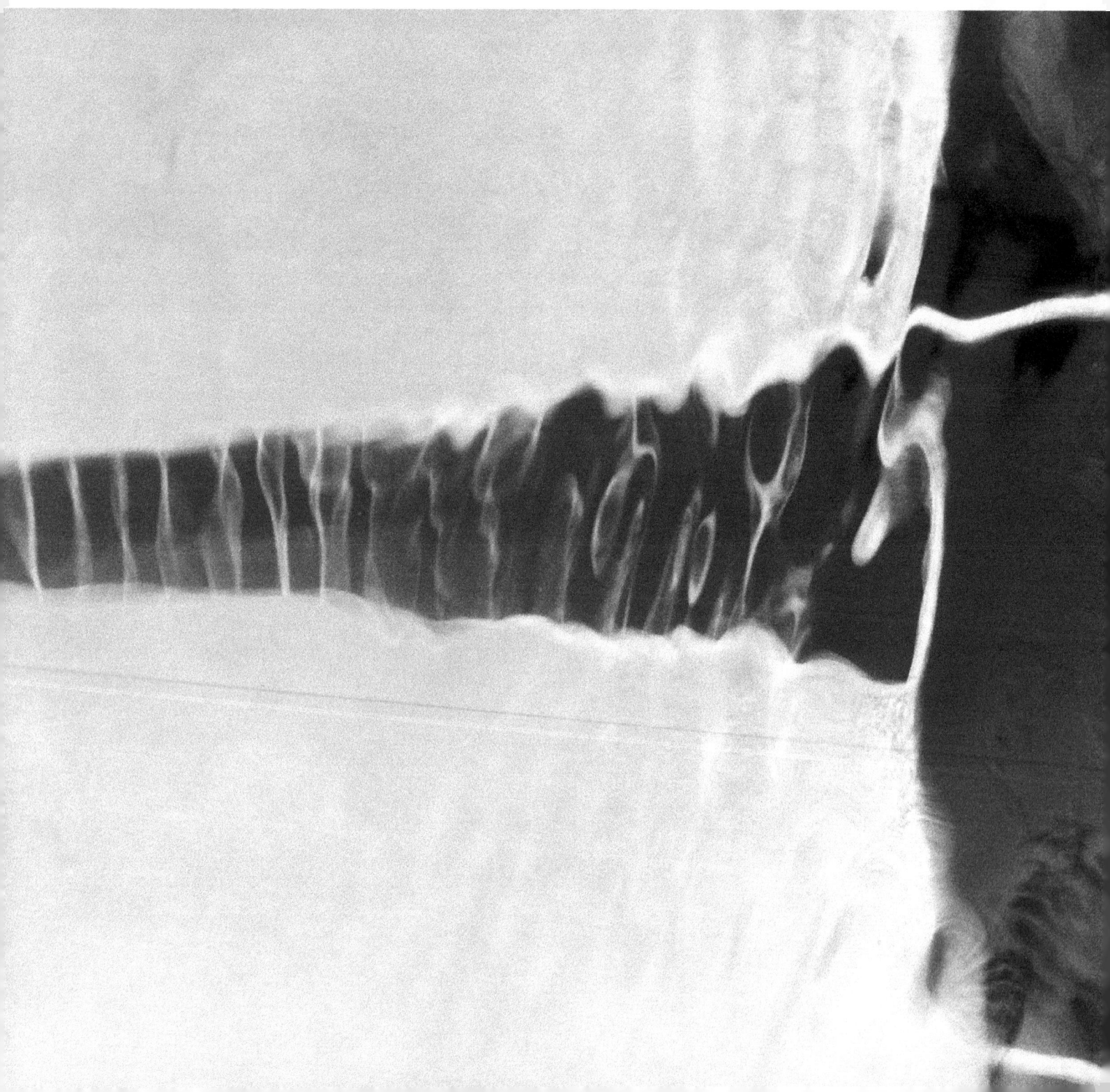

I have been traveling to Cape Canaveral and taking photographs on the beach since I was a child. So when I returned to the Cape to live a few years ago, I resumed my avocation. In the intervening years I have been a theologian and a public spokesperson for the renewal of Jewish ethical life in the face of the challenges presented by Jewish behavior in Israel, especially toward the Palestinians.

For most of my life I balanced my avocation and vocation but then, lo and behold, the ever-infamous Ken Starr became president of my university. What this says about the future of Higher Education is obvious. The result was predictable.

I retired early and began to live full-time at the Cape. These last years have been a time of soul-searching, reevaluation and growth.

Seeking justice and standing in the line of the prophetic tradition I inherit as a Jew is, for me, a no-brainer. Where else can a Jew stand? Still the consequences of speaking truth to power are difficult to live with. Though known for their thundering judgments, the Biblical prophets were individuals with feelings and needs. Today we are witnessing an explosion of the prophetic in our time. We experience the prophets as living breathing individuals who, like other human beings, want justice and peace, beauty and harmony, love and affection.

Wherever we live, whatever faith or culture we come from, to embody the prophetic means exile. My story is part of a larger story. If you're reading these words, no doubt this is part of your story, too. Exiles usually think they are alone but I envision exiles as part of an evolving global community, the New Diaspora. For even if the exile's home is no longer the mainstream of their religious communities, cultures and nations, exiles aren't homeless. Our exilic home is with one another.

Though taken only with an iPhone and for my own enjoyment, others have encouraged me to publish my photographs. When my youngest son, Isaiah, now a graduate student, encouraged me once again, I placed a Facebook plea for help. Tim Gilman, a Christian and a book designer, responded. Our partnership has given birth to this collection.

A dissident Jew and a searching Pentecostal Christian! The New Diaspora in action.

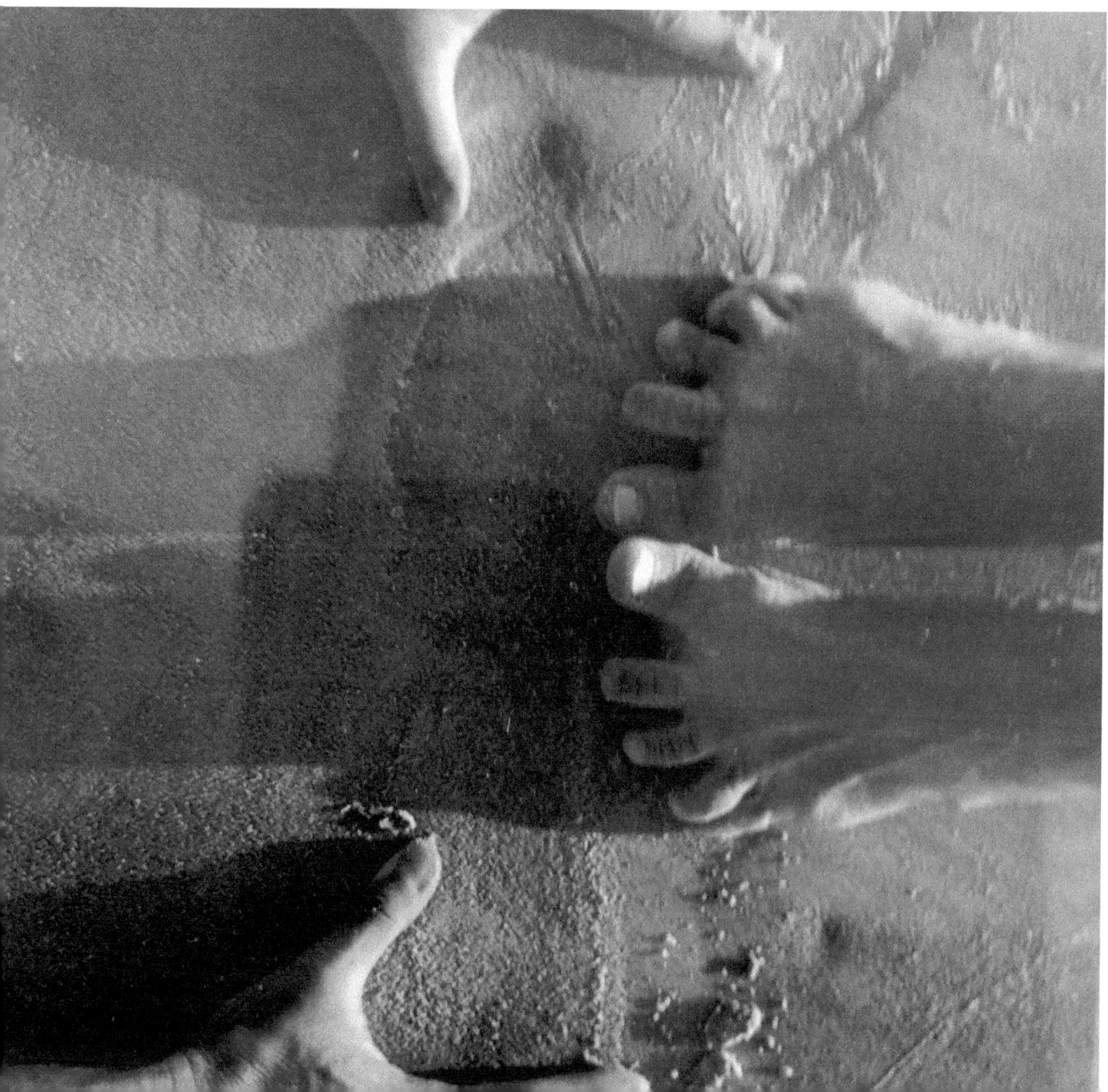

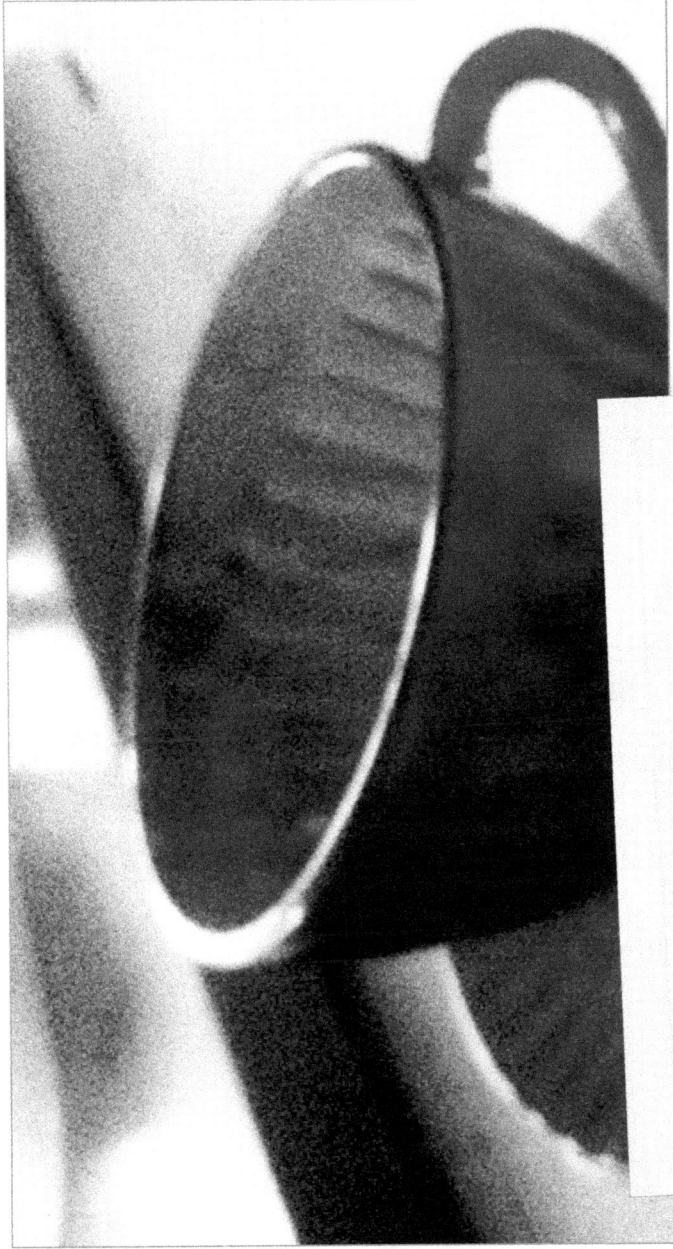

In the middle of the night and at dawn, when the meaning I seek flees, I sometimes scribble notes. "Exile notes" I call them. Then they call me.

I feel the pain of exile. The beauty of the world.
Contradiction. Challenge.

Exile. Where the prophetic is humbled.
Renewed.

The trauma of exile. Devastating. Continuing.

The prophetic is another trauma.
Or perhaps the prophetic is the original trauma.

Shadowed by the prophetic, our lives given over.

As if commanded by God.

To what purpose, the prophetic?

The world continues on its way.
Poverty, wars, torture, corruption, large and small.
Without interruption.

My voice changes nothing.

Exile is bitter:
So I surprise myself.

I learn to make bread to honor the Sabbath.
It isn't Challah - that seems out of reach.
After a few misfires, I succeed. I add honey.
The bread tastes as good as it looks.

On the Sabbath I think of Ezekiel, the psychedelic prophet,
whose call from God is ominous.

God instructs Ezekiel. Go to the people. Tell them they are done
if they don't turn around. Not to worry, they won't. Ezekiel will be reviled
but God will be there for him.

Ezekiel is perplexed; he doesn't like what he hears.
So God commands Ezekiel to eat the text upon which his
doomed mission is foretold.

Ingest, internalize your doom!

Eating the text, Ezekiel is surprised.
The text tastes sweet, just like honey.

I walk the beach at sunrise.
Daily. Like a religious ritual.

The colors of the sky and the ocean change
by the moment. Often in unison, each reflecting the other.

A daily sunrise lesson to be learned over and over again:
A world exists beyond the trauma of exile.

I pay attention to the ordinary and find
beauty in the commonplace.

I see what I experience: fragments, border crossings,
death, unexpected life.

Holding forth, surviving what comes, getting up
off the mat, I regain my balance.

Remaining present.
Fidelity in exile.

Isaiah: "Here I am. Send me."

Where are we sent?
Who sends us?

God is too easy.
God is too difficult.

God is sometimes here, sometimes there, sometimes nowhere to be found.

Exiles know this (unstable/unpredictable) God personally.

So in exile

The prophet carries God's presence - and absence.
The prophet embodies the possibility of God in our world.

Is the "possibility" of God enough?

Dare we claim more?

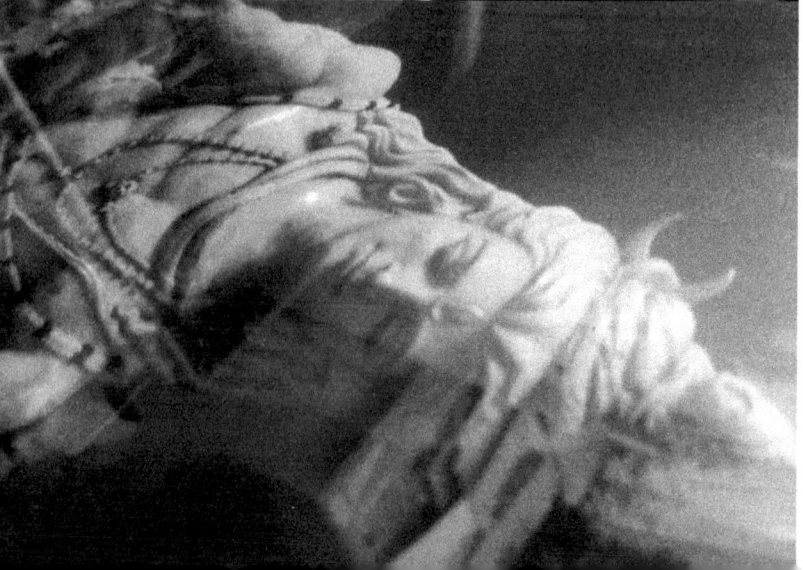

Everywhere I travel injustice and exile *are* close at hand.
My community, the New Diaspora, awaits me.

Everywhere I travel justice and meaning **are** close at hand.
My community, the New Diaspora, awaits me.

Without any one of us we might not make it. Even with
all of us we might not reach the Promised Land.

A new kind of sanctity is indeed a fresh spring, an invention.
If all is kept in proportion and if the order of each thing is preserved, it is almost equivalent
to a new revelation of the universe and of human destiny.

Simone Weil

The Promised Land of justice and equality.
Should we strive for that which we cannot reach?

Our Holy Grail is elusive.

This doesn't mean apathy.
The New Diaspora isn't a rocking chair community.

We need a broader vision, one that doesn't settle for pie
in the ideological or theological sky.

So often our deeper vision eludes us.

Even when it is here, right in front of us.

Dreamscapes. Utopic vibrations.

As our exile deepens, it's easy to harden our hearts.
Still, the heartbeat of the prophetic remains.

The prophetic is always somewhere.
If it isn't here, it's there. If it's there is it also here?

You never know where the prophetic might appear.

Think of the prophetic as a wild card.
Once played, there's no return.

Remain open to the prophetic heartbeat.
It's probably your own.

The common denominator is The emphatic, when the heart beats embody in new indignant.

44

Aaron, my eldest son,
at a thrift store.

Aaron is as he appears - in the
line of the prophets.

Though we live in an age
of'bashing identity and religious belief
or thundering both from the rooftops,
accompanying Aaron, I often ask:

How do we account for
the persistence of the prophetic?

A sound accomplishes nothing; without it life wouldn't last out the instant.

John Cage

My take:

The prophetic accomplishes nothing; without it life wouldn't last out the instant.

What I do, I do not wish blamed on Zen, though without my engagement with Zen
(attendance at lectures by Alan Watts and D. T. Suzuki, reading of the literature)
I doubt whether I would have done what I have done. I am told that Alan Watts has questioned the relation
between my work and Zen. I mention this in order to free Zen of any responsibility for my actions.
I shall continue making them, however.

John Cage

My take:

What I do, I do not wish blamed on the prophetic, though without my engagement with the prophetic
(being raised Jewish, traveling to the poor and oppressed around the world, reading the Bible)
I doubt I have would have done what I have done. I am told that some Jews and Christians have questioned the relation
between my work and the prophetic. I mention this in order to free the prophetic of any responsibility for my actions.
I shall continue making them, however.

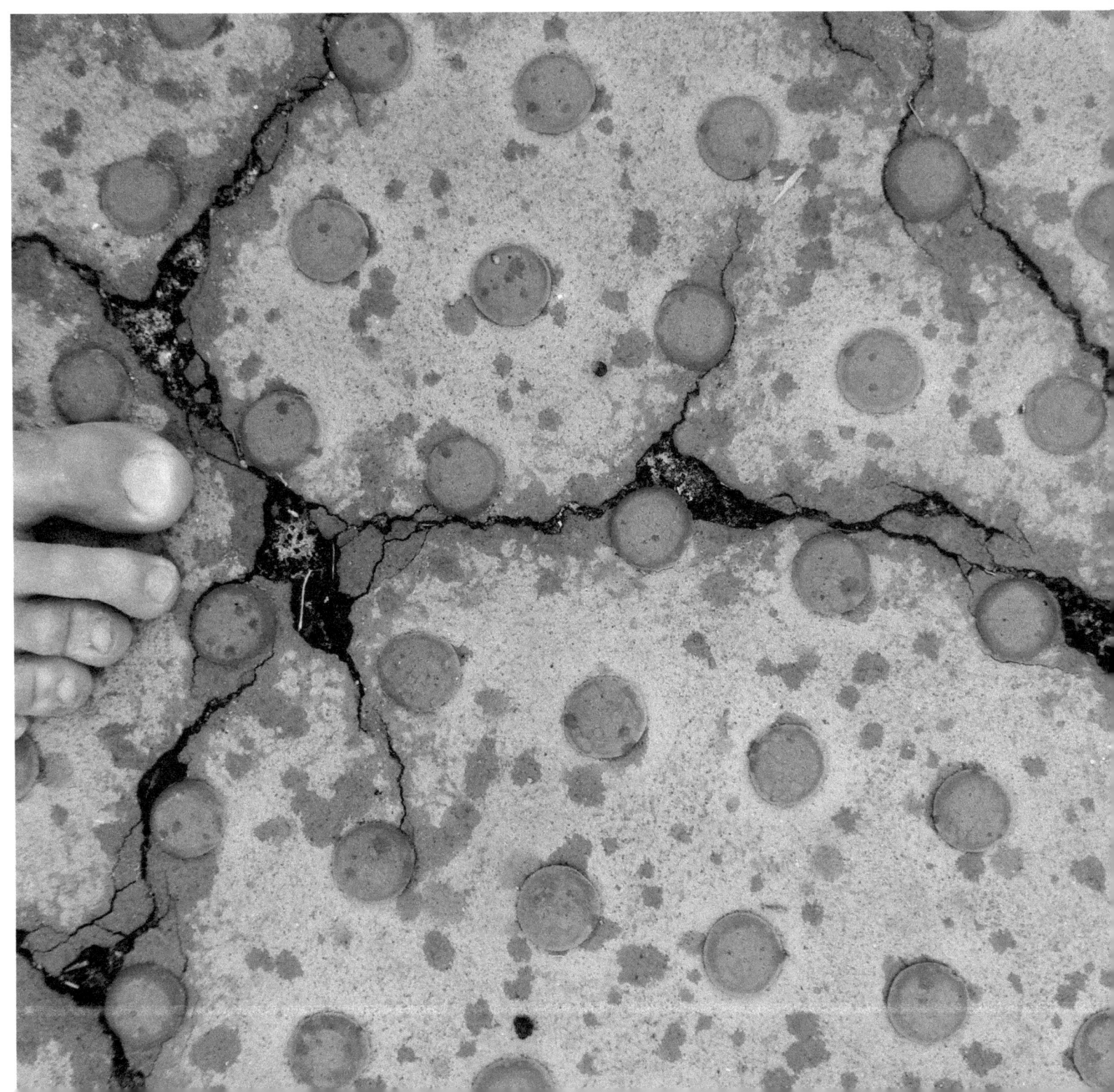

In exile, I think of the observation by Milapera, a Tibetan monk from long ago.
I first found Milapera in the journal of the Catholic monk, Thomas Merton. New Diaspora sharings.

"It is the tradition of the fortunate seekers never to be content with partial practice."

What is partial practice? Is overcoming partial practice the same for everyone, everywhere?
Or, in the New Diaspora, do exiles participate in a communal way of overcoming partial practice?

Perhaps we cannot overcome partial practice once and for all but must keep at it - with others.

Perhaps overcoming partial practice is a lifetime practice of overcoming ourselves.

Is overcoming partial practice easier as we get older?
In exile, I find myself constantly starting again, often from the beginning.

I wrestle with the prophets.

In Cuba, once again with Rabbi Abraham Joshua Heschel who wrote so magnificently about the Biblical prophets.

Heschel is as certain about God as the Biblical prophets he writes about.

Albert Camus, the great French agnostic, asked if one could be a saint without God.

I ask if we can be prophets without God. Or with a diminished God. A God we dare not proclaim too boldly.

In the New Diaspora, can those in the prophetic line encounter each other across the God-Godless divide?

In the New Diaspora what can we honestly say about God?

THE PROPHETS

27 province of
Guantánamo

With an Aborigine name that th... se...
means "land between rivers", Ma...
the easternmost province of Cuba ...
is filled with history, for C... first cult...
town, Baracoa, was fou... is The world
region in 1511. French ... "Guan...
settled in the area a... by Jos...
time developed the co... also k...
coffee plantations in ... ure as ch...
and left their imprin ... live for
d customs, at pr ... nce...
the population.

apital: Guantánam...
a: 6,168 Km²

Gratitude for exile. The greatest challenge.

Solitude and solidarity is the ongoing tension in the life of exiled prophets.

Exiles are alone even when they're together.
Exiles are together even when they're alone.

Breathe justice and compassion alone and together.

Practice exile in the New Diaspora.

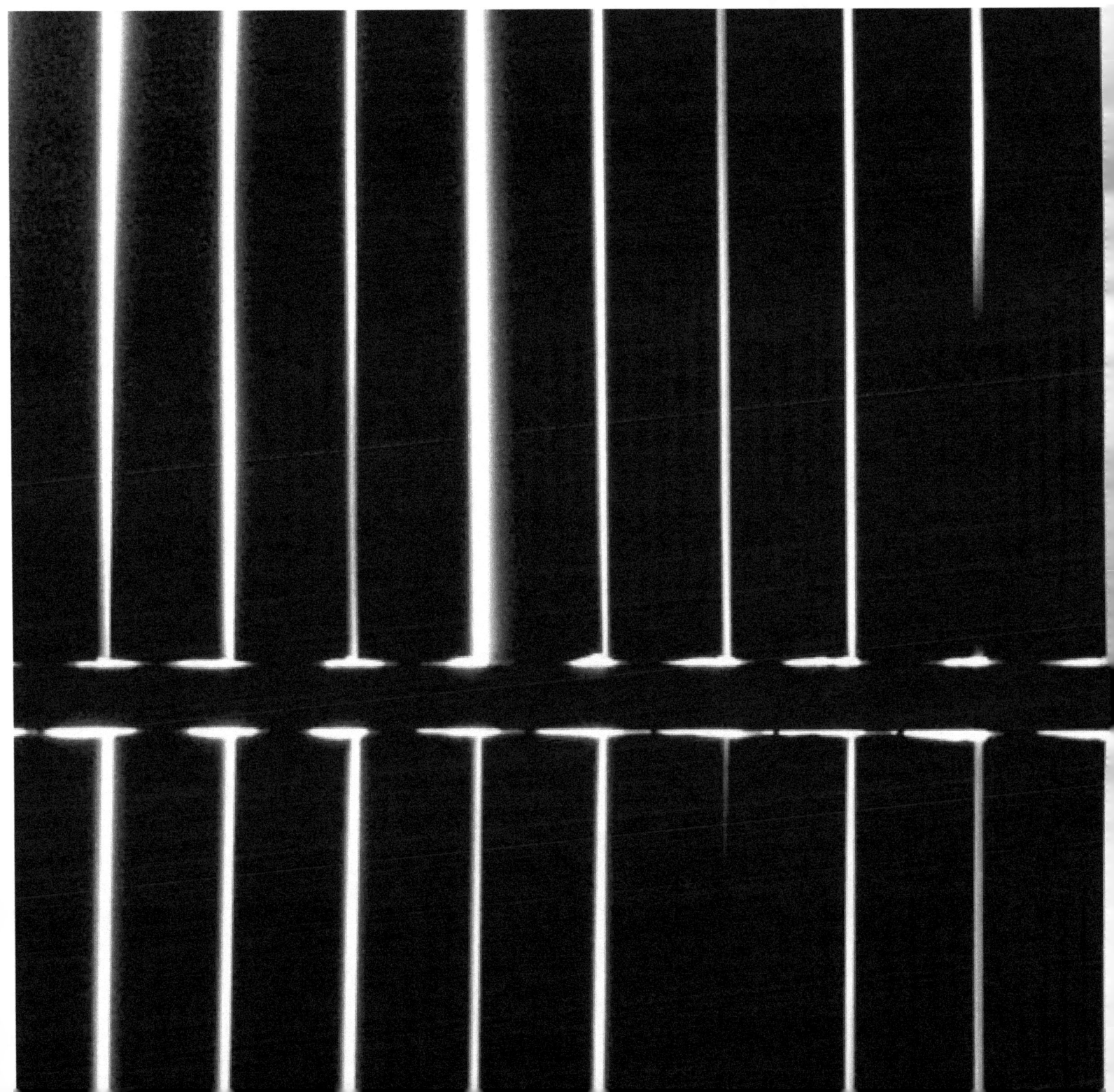

93E5
TYPE
LENGTH
FT.
WEIGHT
LBS.
CLASS
FT.-KIPS
MFG. DATE
CUSTOMER
NEWMARK

About Marc H. Ellis

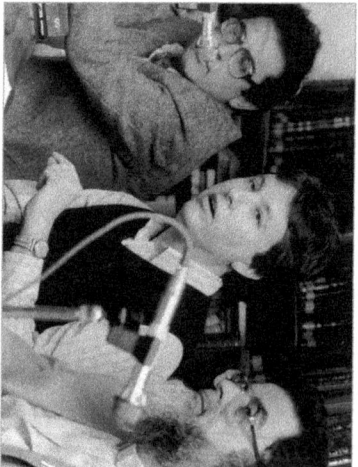

Marc Ellis is a theologian, a historian and now a photographer, who walks the beach each morning at sunrise and continues to write and lecture around the world.

He has two prophetic sons, Aaron and Isaiah, who are now making their way in the world.